Ho
Cookie Decorating
FOR
DUMMIES
MINI EDITION

by Carole Bloom, CCP
and Joe LoCicero

WILEY

John Wiley & Sons, Inc.

Holiday Cake & Cookie Decorating For Dummies, Mini Edition

Published by
John Wiley & Sons, Inc.
111 River St.
Hoboken, NJ 07030-5774
www.wiley.com

For general information on our other products and services, please contact our Customer Care Department within the U.S. at 877-762-2974, outside the U.S. at 317-572-3993, or fax 317-572-4002.

For technical support, please visit www.wiley.com/techsupport.

Wiley also publishes its books in a variety of electronic formats and by print-on-demand. Some content that appears in standard print versions of this book may not be available in other formats. For more information about Wiley products, visit us at www.wiley.com.

ISBN: 978-1-118-13307-1 (pbk); ISBN: 978-1-118-13366-8 (ebk); ISBN: 978-1-118-13367-5 (ebk); ISBN: 978-1-118-13368-2 (ebk)

Manufactured in the United States of America

10 9 8 7 6 5 4 3 2 1

WILEY

Table of Contents

Introduction

● ●

*P*erhaps you've seen the cute and beautifully decorated holiday cakes and cookies on the covers of
magazines as you're waiting in line at the grocery store,
and you think, "I'd like to do that sometime!" The prob-
lem is, you're not sure what you need or where to start.
Well, you've come to the right place!

Baking and decorating holiday-themed cakes and cookies certainly isn't rocket science, but you do need some
basic tools and some basic skills. Once you master the
basics, you can gradually add to your repertoire (and
to your collections of decorator's tools).

In this book, we walk you through everything you need,
such as lists of tools and step-by-step instructions, in
order to become proficient in basic decorating techniques. We provide some specific holiday-themed recipes, and we also provide some general recipes for
cakes, cookies, and frostings, so that you can come up
with your own custom creations.

Icons Used in This Book

We used a few icons to alert you to certain bits of info
throughout the book. Here's what they mean:

This icon marks important information that
you really don't want to forget. If you don't
want to read all the text, at least take a look at
these icons.

When you come across this icon, you've found a tidbit that'll make your life easier (at least as it pertains to baking and decorating).

 As you may have guessed, this icon signals common mistakes and pitfalls and lets you know how to avoid them.

Where to Go from Here

You've got your minibook copy of *Holiday Cake & Cookie Decorating For Dummies* — now what? This minibook is a reference, so if you need information on supplies and techniques, head to chapters 1 and 3. If you already have basic supplies and ingredients on hand, go ahead and skip to the general cake, cookie, and frosting recipes in Chapter 2 or the specific holiday-themed recipes in Chapter 4. Or heck, start with Chapter 1 and read the chapters in order, you rebel. If you want even more advice on baking and decorating cakes and/or cookies, check out the full-size versions of *Cookies For Dummies* and *Cake Decorating For Dummies* — simply head to your local book seller or go to www.dummies.com!

Chapter 1

First Things First: Gathering Your Gear

. . . .

In This Chapter

▶ Making sure your kitchen is ready for baking

▶ Assembling a basic decorating kit

▶ Investing in specialty tools for cakes and cookies

. . . .

ecorating cakes and cookies for the holidays can be extremely fun and rewarding. You can give out treats as gifts or impress your friends at your holiday party. This chapter covers all the essentials you need to get started.

Baking Essentials

You can't very well decorate a holiday cake or cookie without baking it first. Make sure your kitchen is stocked with the basic tools and gadgets discussed in this section.

Measuring cups and spoons

There are two types of measuring cups:

✔ **Dry measuring cups** are used for ingredients such as flour and sugar, and for solid fats.

✔ **Liquid measuring cups** are for — surprise! — liquids, such as water or cooking oil.

Measuring spoons are used for measuring small amounts of both dry and liquid ingredients.

Mixing bowls

Stainless steel, glass, and ceramic bowls are best. They come in a wide variety of sizes, ranging from 1 cup up to 17 quarts. Leave extra room in the bowl for mixing ingredients.

Mixer

There are two main types of mixers — stand and hand-held. Many people prefer a stand mixer because it leaves their hands free for other tasks while the dough or batter is mixing. Hand-held mixers also work fine, though.

Baking pans

Invest in chef-quality pans, which more than make up for the cost with durability and results. As far as pan shapes are concerned, you can get a lot of mileage out of a few basics:

✔ **Rectangular and square:** You should start with one 12-x-18-inch and two 9-x-13-inch rectangular pans, as well as two 10-inch square pans.

✔ **Round:** Invest in two 8-inch or 9-inch rounds to start with.

✔ **Cupcake tins:** You're likely to need two cupcake tins, each one with 12 wells.

▶ **Bundt:** Some bakers like Bundt pans because they can just pour in the batter and not worry about leveling and layering.

Cookie sheets and jelly roll pans

The best cookie sheets are made of heavy-gauge aluminum. They have a shiny surface and a flat rim. Keep at least four on hand so that you don't have to wait for one batch to come out of the oven before arranging the next.

Jelly roll pans are slightly larger than cookie sheets. They have a 1-inch-high rolled rim on all sides that's made to hold batter for cakes or big batches of bar cookies.

You can easily substitute jelly roll pans for cookie sheets.

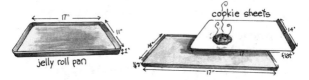

Figure 1-1: Jelly roll pan and cookie sheets.

Parchment paper

You use parchment paper to line your baking pans and cookie sheets. In addition, parchment paper also provides a good practice surface to test out designs beforehand with your frosting-filled pastry bag. Purchase parchment paper either by the roll or in packs of 12-x-16-inch sheets.

Other helpful tools

Following is a list of other helpful tools and gadgets to
have handy when baking holiday cakes and cookies:

- ✔ Chef's knife
- ✔ Cooling racks
- ✔ Dough scraper
- ✔ Flexible-blade spatula
- ✔ Pastry brushes
- ✔ Rolling pin
- ✔ Rubber spatulas
- ✔ Ruler
- ✔ Sifters and strainers
- ✔ Turners
- ✔ Whisk
- ✔ Wooden spoons

Must-Haves for Decorating

Make sure you have the items discussed in this section,
and you're on your way to creating beautifully decorated holiday cakes and cookies.

Essential icing tips

When you're just getting started, you'll repeatedly call
on round tips #1 through #10. You should also gather
the following more-specialized tips:

- ✔ Star tips, such as #16, #18, #21, and #32
- ✔ Basket weave tip, such as #48

✔ Leaf tips, such as #67 and #352

✔ Petal tips, such as #102, #103, #104, and #125

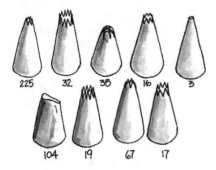

Figure 1-2: Icing tips.

Couplers

To fit a tip onto a pastry bag, you need a coupler, which consists of two parts:

✔ A round plastic cone that you fit inside the pastry bag

✔ A coupler ring that you screw over the tip on the outside of the bag

Couplers are useful when your cake design involves different piping designs in the same color frosting.

Icing spatulas

In the icing spatula arena, most decorators prefer offset or angle-blade spatulas. They're more flexible and give a smoother finish. Get two sizes of the offset kind: a 4-inch one and a 9-inch one. In addition, you'll also get a lot of use out of a straight 8-inch spatula, which is particularly good for crumb coating a cake.

Paper goods, pastry bags, and more

The following items should be on hand in your pantry:

- ✔ **Wax paper:** Placing wax paper strips under the edge of the cake before you decorate and then removing them after you're done keeps your board free of any smudges or frosting drips.

- ✔ **Plastic tumblers:** Clear, plastic tumblers are great for holding frosting-filled pastry bags upright or for holding empty bags upright while you fill them with frosting.

- ✔ **Paper bowls:** Mixing frosting and colors in paper bowls means easy cleanup.

- ✔ **Plastic spoons:** Mixing frosting and colors with plastic spoons is a great way to cut down on your cleanup time.

- ✔ **Disposable pastry bags:** It's easier to toss a frosting bag away after you're done using it rather than try to clean out the excess frosting.

- ✔ **Cardboard rounds and squares:** Typically, you set each layer of a cake on a cardboard round or square to provide stability to the cake.

- ✔ **Food coloring:** You'll need various colors to tint your frostings and icings.

Specialty Tools

If you really get serious about decorating cakes or
cookies for the holidays and beyond, you'll want to
consider investing in some specialty tools, such as the
ones discussed in the following sections.

For cakes

The tools covered in this section help you refine your
cake design and allow for a more polished and profes-
sional look.

Leveler

Typically, this apparatus consists of a sharp blade or
wire stretched between two short steel poles with a
handle on the top. You adjust the blade to the height of
your cake top, set the poles on your work surface, and
slide the blade across the cake, taking off just enough
to make the entire layer level.

Turntable

With this device, your cake sits on a platform that rests
on a rotating wheel of sorts. You can stay in one position while you spin your cake around to frost and decorate it on all sides.

Bench scraper

Usually about 6 inches long, a bench scraper is an ideal
tool for smoothing out the frosting on a cake's sides or
circumference.

Decorating comb

Drawing it over a layer of frosting creates evenly
spaced rows, lines, and V-shaped patterns across the
top of a cake or along its sides.

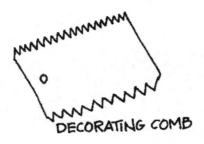

Figure 1-3: A decorating comb is a great tool for adding texture to frosting.

For cookies

Some cookie recipes require specialized tools. You don't have to buy all the tools at once. Instead, you can acquire them over time as you try new and exciting recipes.

Cookie cutters

Buy a few basic cookie cutters to get started and add to your collection when the mood strikes you. Plenty of holiday and special-occasion cookie cutters are available.

Cookie press

Sometimes called a cookie gun, a cookie press has a cylindrical barrel with several different round templates or nozzles that fit at one end. At the other end is a trigger or plunger mechanism that forces the soft cookie dough out through the template, forming different shapes.

Chapter 2

Basic Recipes for Cakes, Cookies, Frostings, and Icings

• •

In This Chapter
▶ Baking up white cake and yellow cake
▶ Creating classics with sugar cookies and gingerbread
▶ Whipping up versatile frostings and icings

• •

*I*n order to decorate a cake or cookie, you have to bake something first. It also helps to have some frosting or icing ready. This chapter arms you with basic recipes that can become the foundation of any number of holiday-themed cakes or cookies, including the ones found in Chapter 4 of this book.

Versatile Cakes and Cookies

In this section, you find two basic cake recipes — a white cake and a yellow. The possibilities are endless with either of these cakes as your base. You also find a recipe for classic rolled sugar cookies, which can be cut into any holiday-themed shaped.

A Most Excellent White Cake

This delicious white cake bakes up high-and-mighty and is a staple for all kinds of celebrations.

Tools: *Two 9-inch round cake pans*

Preparation time: *15 minutes*

Baking time: *45 minutes*

Yield: *12 servings*

Ingredients

4½ cups sifted cake flour

¾ teaspoon salt

1 tablespoon plus 1 teaspoon baking powder

7 egg whites

2 cups whole milk

9 tablespoons unsalted butter, slightly softened and cut into ½-inch pieces

2½ cups granulated white sugar

1½ teaspoons pure vanilla extract

Directions

1 Preheat the oven to 350 degrees F. Grease and flour two 9-inch round cake pans, and set aside.

2 In a large bowl, sift the salt and baking powder into the cake flour, and stir the mixture with a balloon whisk.

3 In a medium bowl, break up the egg whites with a fork, add the milk, and mix together lightly.

4 In a large bowl, cream the butter. Add the sugar, and continue beating until light and fluffy. Add the vanilla, and continue beating.

5 Alternately add the flour and egg white mixture to the butter mixture, beginning and ending with the flour. Scrape down the sides of the bowl twice during beating. Stop beating when the last portion of flour is just blended into the mixture.

6 Pour the batter into the prepared pans, and bake for 45 minutes, or until a cake tester inserted in the center of the cake comes out with moist crumbs attached.

7 Cool the cakes in the pans on wire racks for 10 minutes. Run a knife around the edges, and then invert the cakes onto racks to cool completely.

Delicious Yellow Cake

Another staple for your repertoire, this yellow cake is popular for all occasions and pairs well with buttercream and milk chocolate frosting, which I cover later in this chapter.

Tools: *Two 9-inch round cake pans*

Preparation time: *15 minutes*

Baking time: *40 minutes*

Yield: *12 servings*

Ingredients

1 tablespoon baking powder

½ teaspoon salt

3½ cups sifted cake flour

1¼ cups butter, at room temperature and cut into ½-inch pieces

2 cups granulated white sugar

1 teaspoon pure vanilla extract

5 eggs

1 cup whole milk

Directions

1 Preheat the oven to 350 degrees F. Grease and flour two 9-inch round cake pans, and set aside.

2 In a large bowl, sift together the baking powder and salt. Then whisk in the cake flour.

3 In a large bowl, cream the butter. Add the sugar, and beat until light and fluffy. Add the vanilla, and continue beating.

4 Add the eggs to the butter mixture, one at a time, beating well after each addition.

5 With the mixer set on low speed, add the flour mixture and the milk to the egg mixture alternately, beginning and ending with the flour. Each addition should be mixed until just combined. Scrape down the sides of the bowl twice during beating.

6 Pour the batter into the prepared pans, and bake for 35 to 40 minutes, or until the cake springs back when lightly touched and a cake tester inserted in the center of the cake comes out with moist crumbs attached.

7 Cool the cakes in the pans on wire racks for 10 minutes. Run a knife around the edges, and then invert the cakes onto racks to cool completely.

Rolled Sugar Cookies

Crisp sugar cookies are all-time favorites. You can garnish them with *nonpareils,* which are tiny multi-colored sugar pellets. You can make ornaments by poking a hole near the top before baking. After they're cool, string a decorative ribbon through the hole.

Tools: *Rolling pin, cookie cutters, paper pastry cone (optional), food processor*

Preparation time: *1½ hours; includes chilling*

Baking time: *8 minutes*

Yield: *4 dozen*

Ingredients

2½ cups all-purpose flour

2 teaspoons baking powder

Pinch of salt

1 cup superfine sugar

¼ cup confectioners' sugar

½ cup plus 2 tablespoons (1¼ sticks) unsalted butter, softened

1 egg

1½ teaspoons vanilla extract

Directions

1 Combine flour, baking powder, salt, superfine sugar, and confectioners' sugar in the work bowl of a food processor fitted with the steel blade. Pulse briefly to blend. Cut the butter into small pieces and add. Pulse until the butter is cut into very tiny

pieces. In a small bowl, lightly beat the egg with the vanilla and add to the butter mixture. Pulse until the dough forms a ball, about 30 seconds. Wrap tightly in plastic and chill, at least 2 hours.

(To mix the dough using a mixer and bowl, beat the butter until fluffy, about 2 minutes. Sift the confectioners' sugar and add to the butter with the superfine sugar. Cream together well. Lightly beat the egg with the vanilla extract and add. Blend well. Combine the flour, baking powder, and salt and add to the mixture in three stages, blending well after each addition. Proceed to wrap and chill the dough.)

2 Preheat the oven to 375 degrees F. Line a cookie sheet with parchment paper.

3 Divide the dough in two and roll each section between sheets of lightly floured wax paper to a thickness of ½ inch. Gently peel off the wax paper and use a variety of cookie cutters to shape the dough. Transfer the cookies to the cookie sheet, leaving 2 inches between the cookies. If desired, sprinkle crystal sugar or nonpareils over the cookies.

4 Bake for 8 to 10 minutes, until the cookies are firm. Remove the cookie sheet from the oven and transfer the cookies from the parchment to cooling racks.

Per serving: *Calories 64 (From Fat 23); Fat 3g (Saturated 2g); Cholesterol 11mg; Sodium 21mg; Carbohydrate 10g (Dietary Fiber 0g); Protein 1g.*

Gingerbread

Gingerbread is especially popular in the fall and during the holidays. This gingerbread is delicious served warm with whipped cream.

Preparation time: *20 minutes*

Baking time: *45 minutes*

Yield: *16 squares*

Ingredients

2½ cups all-purpose flour

2 teaspoons baking powder

1 tablespoon ground ginger

1 teaspoon ground cinnamon

½ teaspoon ground cloves

¼ teaspoon ground nutmeg

¼ teaspoon salt

½ cup (1 stick) unsalted butter, at room temperature

¼ cup light brown sugar

¼ cup sugar

2 eggs, lightly beaten

1 cup dark molasses

1 cup boiling water

Directions

1 Preheat the oven to 375 degrees F. Prepare an 8x8x2-inch baking pan by generously buttering with 1 tablespoon of butter. Dust pan with 1 tablespoon of flour and shake out the excess.

2 Sift the flour, baking soda, ginger, cinnamon, cloves, and nutmeg together on a large piece of wax paper and then blend in the salt. Set this mixture aside briefly.

3 Using a mixer, beat the butter in a large mixing bowl until it's soft and fluffy, about 2 minutes. Add the brown sugar and sugar and continue to beat until the mixture is well blended, about 2 more minutes. Stop and scrape down the sides of the bowl with a rubber spatula two times.

4 Blend in the eggs and the molasses, beating well, and then add the boiling water. Scrape down the bottom and sides of the bowl. With the mixer on low speed, add the dry ingredients from Step 2 in several small batches, beating to blend well after each addition.

5 Spread the mixture in the prepared pan and bake for 45 minutes, until a cake tester inserted in the center comes out clean.

6 Remove the pan from the oven and cool on a rack. Cut the gingerbread into squares and serve. Store tightly wrapped in foil at room temperature for up to 4 days. Freeze for longer storage.

Per serving: Calories 213 (From Fat 60); Fat 7g (Saturated 4g); Cholesterol 42mg; Sodium 212mg; Carbohydrate 36g (Dietary Fiber 1g); Protein 3g.

Fabulous Frostings and Icings

In this section, you find some of the most common and most versatile frostings and icings for cakes and cookies.

Buttercream Frosting

The most versatile of the lot, buttercream frosting is sure to be an essential component of your frosting repertoire. It spreads and pipes wonderfully, and because of its lustrous, white appearance, you can tint it to exactly the color you want.

Tools: *Electric mixer, paddle attachment*

Preparation time: *10 minutes*

Yield: *2 cups*

Ingredients

1 cup unsalted butter, softened

1 teaspoon pure vanilla extract

3¾ cups confectioners' sugar, sifted

¼ cup milk

Directions

1 In a large bowl, beat the butter and vanilla on medium speed for about 30 seconds.

2 Gradually add half the sugar, beating well.

3 Beat in the milk, and then add the remaining sugar. Continue beating until the frosting is smooth and creamy and reaches the desired consistency.

Stiff Decorator Frosting

If you have a lot of ground to cover decorating-wise on your cake, or if the intricacy of the design will require time and patience, this frosting is an excellent choice because it holds its shape for a long time, without hardening immediately, allowing you the latitude to futz with the decorating without it "melting."

Tools: *Electric mixer, paddle attachment*

Preparation time: *10 minutes*

Yield: *4 cups*

Ingredients

7 cups sifted confectioners' sugar

¾ cup all-vegetable shortening

⅓ cup whole milk

¼ teaspoon almond extract

Directions

1 Combine the sugar and shortening in the bowl of an electric mixer. Beat on low speed until the ingredients start to come together. Beat in the almond extract.

2 Gradually add the whole milk as you increase the mixing speed until the frosting is smooth and creamy. If necessary, beat in a few more drops of milk until you reach the desired consistency, which should be holding firm but pliable peaks.

Royal Icing

Use this icing for drawing, filling in, and accenting designs and forms on cakes. It also works well for decorating cookies.

Preparation time: *5 minutes*

Yield: *2 cups*

Ingredients

4 cups sifted confectioners' sugar

¾ cup pasteurized egg whites

1 tablespoon fresh-squeezed lemon juice

Directions

1 In a large bowl, combine all the ingredients.

2 Beat the mixture with a stand or a hand-mixer until the icing holds its shape and isn't runny. If it's too thin for piping, add more sugar 1 tablespoon at a time and continue mixing until it reaches the desired consistency.

Tip: *To tint the icing several different colors, pour the icing into separate bowls, and then add and adjust coloring gels with a toothpick or by squeezing a few drops of color at a time into the icing.*

Milk Chocolate Frosting

This versatile frosting adds a nice (and decadent) depth to the Most Excellent White Cake (listed earlier in this chapter), and it amps up the flavor as a filling for the Delicious Yellow Cake, too. Whatever cake you decide to pair it with, know that it's always a hit with candy bar connoisseurs.

Tools: *Electric mixer, paddle attachment*

Preparation time: *10 minutes*

Yield: *About 2 cups*

Ingredients

½ cup unsalted butter, softened

¼ cup sifted unsweetened cocoa powder

2 cups sifted confectioners' sugar

3 tablespoons heavy whipping cream

Directions

1 In the bowl of an electric mixer, beat the butter until fluffy.

2 Add the cocoa powder and sugar, and beat on medium speed to combine.

3 Gradually add in the whipping cream, beating until the frosting is creamy. If necessary, beat in additional cream one drop at a time until the frosting reaches the desired consistency to be perfectly spreadable.

Cream Cheese Frosting

This frosting pairs exceptionally well with a host of cakes, including Red Velvet Cake (Chapter 4). With a consistency and color similar to buttercream, it's also an ideal frosting for piping. *Note:* For optimal flavor and texture, don't use reduced fat cream cheese or Neufchatel cheese in this recipe.

Tools: Electric mixer, paddle attachment

Preparation time: 10 minutes

Yield: 2 cups

Ingredients

8-ounce package cream cheese, softened

$\frac{1}{2}$ cup unsalted butter, softened

$3\frac{3}{4}$ cup confectioners' sugar, sifted

1 teaspoon pure vanilla extract

Directions

1 In a large bowl, cream the butter and cream cheese on medium speed until combined and fluffy.

2 Set the mixer on low speed, and add the confectioners' sugar to the creamed mixture in batches. After all the sugar is incorporated, increase to medium speed to thoroughly mix the ingredients.

3 Add the vanilla, and continue beating until combined.

Vary It!: For a peppermint cream cheese frosting, substitute $\frac{1}{2}$ teaspoon peppermint flavoring for the vanilla. For a lemon cream cheese frosting, substitute $\frac{1}{2}$ teaspoon lemon flavoring for the vanilla.

Chapter 3

Frosting and Piping Techniques

- -

In This Chapter

▶ Grasping proper frosting techniques

▶ Getting your pastry bag ready for piping

▶ Practicing some basic piping techniques

- -

*I*n order to master just about any holiday cake or cookie decoration, you first have to master proper frosting and piping techniques. That's what this chapter is all about.

Frosting with Finesse

Frosting a cake is more than just slapping on a layer of sweet confection and calling it a day. Frosting the right way requires time, tools, and attention to detail. The most important tools you should have on hand are different sized icing spatulas, a pastry brush, and a decorating turntable.

 When you have your plain or colored frosting ready to apply to your cake, check its consistency. If the frosting is too thick, you'll tear the cake as you attempt to spread the frosting. To thin out your frosting, return it to the mixer and add some milk (a teaspoon at a time) until it's the right spreadable consistency. If the frosting is too thin, it will run or puddle, leaving you with incomplete and unattractive coverage. If it was once the right consistency, it probably has just gotten too warm, so put it in the refrigerator for a few minutes to allow it to thicken.

Follow these steps to frost a two-layer, 9-inch round cake. These guidelines are easily adaptable to other cake sizes:

1. **Gather all the tools you'll need to frost: wax paper, offset icing spatula, frosting knife, silicone brush, and (preferably) a pedestal that has a rotating round top.**

2. **Place four 2-x-8-inch strips of wax paper around the board your cake will sit on for presentation. Place the first layer of the leveled cake on the board, and then put the board on the pedestal.**

3. **With the silicone brush, sweep all excess crumbs off your cake layer.**

4. **Use the frosting knife to scoop about ½ cup of frosting onto the cake layer. With the offset icing spatula, spread the frosting evenly and smoothly on the top of the cake only. The initial crumb coat (discussed a little later) will be a scant, thin layer of frosting; think of it as providing a "protective seal" for your cake. The subsequent coat will be quite thicker, about ¼-inch to ⅜-inch thick.**

A frosting knife is a specialty tool with a generous blade that allows you to heap frosting onto your cake layers easily. You can also use a rubber spatula to scoop frosting out onto your cake.

5. **Place the second cake layer — flat side up — on top of the first. Again, sweep any excess crumbs off the top and sides of cake.**

6. **Use the frosting knife to scoop ½ cup of frosting on top of the cake, and use the offset spatula to spread it out in even strokes to be a thin seal for the crumb coat, and a ¼- to ⅜-inch thickness for the second coat. Use excess frosting from the top of the cake to frost the sides of the cake, rotating the pedestal as you use the flat edge of the spatula for a smooth, even finish. Add more frosting from the bowl as necessary to cover the sides with a thin layer of frosting.**

   This first layer of frosting is the crumb coat (which I explain in the next section). The cake needs to be refrigerated for at least 1 hour before you apply the final frosting coat.

7. **For the final coat of frosting on the cake's top and sides, repeat Step 6 but with a thicker layer of frosting. Keep adding and subtracting frosting until you have the smooth, finished look that you desire.**

Taking care to crumb coat

Have you ever noticed that some cakes have bits of crumbs in the frosting? Unless you're going for the speckled look, applying a crumb coat to your cake will stop those crumbs in their tracks. The thin layer of frosting provides protection to keep crumbs out of your decorations and the frosting layer that your party-goers see. This one simple step ensures professional-looking results for your frosted cake. Follow these steps to crumb coat your cake:

1. **After your cake has cooled completely, level it and brush off any excess crumbs.**

2. **Using a wide icing spatula, spread a thin layer of frosting over the top and all sides of the cake.**

3. **Refrigerate the cake for at least 1 hour.**

   Chilling the cake allows the frosting to crust and seal in any crumbs that may still be left on your prepared cake.

Thanks to the crumb coat, when you apply the second coat of frosting to the cake, you don't have to worry about any crumbs mixing in with the frosting. You're guaranteed to get a clean, polished presentation.

Smoothing out the frosting

Some cake designs benefit from a textured coat of frosting, but many bakers and cake decorators crave the smooth look that wedding and other elaborate cakes tend to sport.

Make the process of frosting your cake a bit easier by setting your cake board on a sturdy surface. If necessary, place it on damp kitchen towels to keep it from shifting as you work. If you're frosting a round cake, consider putting it on a turntable that you can spin as you frost.

You have a few options to go about getting a smooth coat of frosting on your cake.

✔ **Use an icing spatula.** Perhaps you grew up watching a parent or grandmother frost cakes using a butter knife. That was fine then, but for best results, bring in an icing spatula! The spatula flattens out the frosting and creates sharp edges, particularly at the corners of a square or rectangular cake.

Put some frosting on your cake and then slide the spatula's flat edge across the top of the cake in an even, continuous motion. Then run the spatula over each side of the cake, working your way around.

✔ **Use a piece of parchment paper or a paper towel.** Press the paper onto the frosting and then lift it off, or carefully pull it across the surface of the cake. Work on the top of the cake first, and then the sides.

✔ **Use the straight edge of a ruler or strip of stiff, clean cardboard or poster board.** Draw the straight edge across the cake, collecting the excess frosting and leaving a smooth surface in your wake. Perform this method on the top of the cake first, then repeat on the sides.

If you try these methods and still don't achieve the smooth results you want, refrigerate your cake to let the frosting harden a bit. Then try using the icing spatula again or a bench scraper to even out the frosting.

Preparing to Pipe

Gather your pastry bags, tips, and couplers (refer to Chapter 1) and get ready to have some fun!

Outfitting a pastry bag

Follow these instructions to outfit a pastry bag with the proper hardware and your beautifully tinted frosting:

1. **Prepare one tall plastic cup (16 ounces or so) for each pastry bag you plan to fill. For each cup, moisten a paper towel, fold it into a square, and place it in the bottom of the cup.**

2. **Drop a cone-shaped coupler into a pastry bag and position it so that the small end of the coupler fits into the point of the bag. Snip off the end of the bag only to the point that the cone is flush with the opening.**

3. **Insert an icing tip into the coupler ring, and screw the coupler ring onto the pastry bag.**

4. **Fold down the wide end of the bag to make a 2-inch cuff. Set the bag upright in the tall cup, and fold the cuff over the rim of the cup.**

   The cuff keeps the bag neat.

5. **Using the large icing spatula, transfer 1/2 cup to 2/3 cup of frosting to the bag.**

   These amounts are great for practicing. When you're decorating a cake, you want to fill the bag half-full. Any more than that and frosting will ooze out as you pipe.

6. **Roll the cuff back up, and secure the bag with a locking bag clip.**

A bag clip is similar to a chip bag clip that snaps into place.

Holding the bag

Before you begin piping, remove the bag clip that you affixed to the bag. As you work, you'll keep the bag sealed with your guiding hand loosely gripped around it.

When piping, apply pressure to the bag with your dominant hand and guide the bag with your other hand. To hold the bag while decorating, curl four fingers of your nondominant hand around the top of the bag, and apply even pressure with your dominant hand at the tip end to squeeze frosting through the tip. The frosting will continue coming out until you stop squeezing. As you decorate, periodically squeeze frosting from the top of the bag down toward the tip so that you get a steady flow of frosting and therefore a neater execution of your design.

Piping Dots, Rosettes, and More

All dots, rosettes, shells, stars, and leaves are not created equal. Different tips turn out different designs in different sizes, making it easy to create variations on popular decorations. See Figure 3-1.

To pipe a dot, you simply hold your bag at a 90-degree angle, squeeze the frosting out, stop squeezing, lift up your tip, and move on. If tips intimidate you, start with the open round tips in the #1 to #11 range, which are easy to maneuver.

Rosettes, shells, stars, and leaves may take a bit more practice and patience than dots, but you'll be crafting them in no time as well.

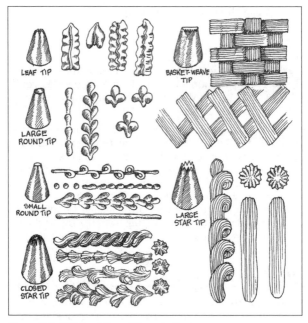

Figure 3-1: Different tips, different effects.

Rosettes

To make rosettes:

1. **Hold the bag at a 90-degree angle to the surface, about ⅛ inch above it.**

2. **Squeeze the pastry bag and hold the tip in place briefly before moving the tip around to the right in a short circular motion.**

3. Stop squeezing just before you reach the original starting point, and pull the tip away.

Shells

To make shells:

1. Hold the bag at a 45-degree angle to the surface, slightly above the surface.

2. Squeeze the pastry bag until the frosting builds up and fans out into a base as you lift the tip up slightly.

3. Relax pressure as you lower the tip, just until it touches the surface.

4. Release the pressure on the bag. Pull the tip away without lifting it off the surface, drawing the shell to a point.

For a row of shells, place the head of one shell on the tail of the shell that precedes it. For larger shells, increase your piping pressure. For smaller shells, use less pressure.

Stars

To make stars:

1. Hold the bag at a 90-degree angle to the surface, about ⅛ inch above it.

2. Squeeze the pastry bag until a star forms. Release the pressure, and pull the tip away at a 90-degree angle. To get a well-defined star, make sure that you stop squeezing before you pull the tip away.

Leaves

To make leaves:

1. Hold the pastry bag at a 45-degree angle to the surface, touching the tip to the surface.

2. Squeeze the pastry bag, drawing the tip into a leaf shape, lessening pressure as you move to the leaf's point.

3. Release pressure on the bag, and bring the leaf out to a point.

Chapter 4

Holiday Cake and Cookie Recipes

• •

In This Chapter

▶ Celebrating fall festivities

▶ Warming hearts during winter holidays

• •

*I*n this chapter, you find recipes for cakes and cookies that make fabulous additions to fall and winter celebrations, as well as great gifts.

Cakes and Cookies for Fall Holidays

Fall marks the beginning of the holiday season and is a time for friends and fun. Bring any of these cakes and cookies to a party, and you're sure to impress!

Jack-O'-Lantern Cake

Here's a jack-o'-lantern that doesn't have to be
scooped out! A fluted Bundt pan creates a realistic
look, and the Brown Sugar Cake fits the tenor of
October . . . but is delicious year-round.

Tools: *Two 10-fluted Bundt pans, #10 icing tip*

Preparation time: *20 minutes*

Baking time: *50 minutes plus 30 minutes for cooling*

Decoration time: *35 minutes plus 1 hour for
refrigeration*

Yield: *24 servings*

Ingredients

For the cake

2 batches Brown Sugar Cake batter (recipe follows)

For the frosting

2 batches Buttercream Frosting (see Chapter 2)

For the decorations

Black food coloring gel

Leaf green food coloring gel

Sunset orange food coloring gel

Banana, unpeeled

Directions

Preparing the cake

1 Prepare the Brown Sugar Cake batter according to
the recipe that follows. However, with two pans in

the oven, rotate the pans midway through the baking time.

2 Let the cakes cool in the pans for at least 10 minutes, and then run a knife around the edges. Invert the cakes onto cooling racks, and then invert them again so that they're right side up.

3 After the cakes are completely cool, apply a crumb coat (thin layer) of buttercream frosting, and refrigerate them for 1 hour.

Decorating the cake

1 Divide and tint the buttercream frosting as follows: 1 cup black, ½ cup leaf green, and the remainder orange.

2 Turn one cake upside down, and frost it with orange buttercream. Put the other cake on top of it, right side up, and frost the entire cake orange. With the last coat of frosting, frost the cake with a downward motion to create the striations found on a real pumpkin.

3 Outfit a pastry bag with a coupler, a #10 tip, and black frosting. On the side of the pumpkin, pipe two triangles for the eyes, one triangle for the nose, and a series of smaller triangles for the mouth.

4 Cut the banana in half, and cover it with green frosting. Insert it stem side up into the hole at the top of the pumpkin.

Brown Sugar Cake

This is one of my most favorite and most requested cakes. Its caramel flavor also pairs well with milk chocolate frosting (see Chapter 2 for a recipe).

Preparation time: *20 minutes*

Baking time: *50 minutes*

Ingredients

3¾ cups sifted cake flour

1½ teaspoons baking soda

2¼ cups vegetable oil

2¼ cups dark brown sugar

3 eggs

1½ teaspoons pure vanilla extract

1½ cups buttermilk

Directions

1 Preheat the oven to 350 degrees F. Spray a Bundt pan with baking spray that contains flour, and set it aside.

2 In a medium bowl, combine the cake flour and baking soda. Stir them together with a balloon whisk.

3 In a large mixing bowl, combine the oil and sugar, and beat the mixture until blended.

4 Add the eggs to the oil and sugar mixture, one at a time, beating well after each addition. Add the vanilla, and beat to blend.

5 Add the flour in four additions, alternating with the buttermilk. (Begin and end with the flour.) Mix each flour addition just until blended.

6 Pour the batter into the prepared pan, and bake for 50 minutes, or until a cake tester inserted in the center comes out with moist crumbs attached.

7 Let the cake cool in the pan for 10 minutes before inverting it onto a cooling rack to cool completely.

Apricot-Almond Thumbprints

These cookies are beautiful, tasty, and perfect for fall and winter festivities.

Preparation time: 20 minutes

Baking time: 16–18 minutes

Yield: 4 dozen

Ingredients

2 cups all-purpose flour

½ teaspoon baking powder

1 teaspoon ground cinnamon

1 cup (2 sticks) unsalted butter, softened

⅓ cup sugar

¼ cup light brown sugar

2 eggs

1 teaspoon vanilla extract

1 teaspoon almond extract

1½ cups finely chopped toasted almonds

½ cup apricot preserves

Directions

1 Preheat the oven to 350 degrees F. Line a cookie sheet with parchment paper.

2 Sift together the flour, baking powder, and cinnamon. Set aside. Using a mixer, beat the butter in a large mixing bowl until fluffy, about 1 minute. Add the sugar and brown sugar and mix together until smooth.

3 Separate the eggs and lightly beat the egg yolks
with the vanilla and almond extracts. Add to the
butter mixture and blend thoroughly. Add the flour
mixture in three stages, blending well after each
addition. Stop and scrape down the sides of the
bowl occasionally. Stir in ½ cup almonds and blend
well. Gather the dough into a disk, cover tightly in
plastic wrap, and chill for about 30 minutes, until
firm but still pliable.

4 Place the egg whites in a small bowl and stir lightly.
Place the remaining 1 cup almonds in another small
bowl. Break off walnut-size pieces of the dough and
roll into balls. Coat the balls with the egg white
and then roll in the almonds, coating completely.
Place the balls on the cookie sheet, with 1 inch
between them. Use your thumb to press an indentation into the center of each ball. Place about
½ teaspoon of preserves in each indentation.

5 Bake for 16 to 18 minutes, until golden and set.
Remove the cookie sheet from the oven and transfer the cookies to racks to cool. Store in a single
layer between sheets of wax paper in an airtight
container at room temperature for 3 days.

Per serving: Calories 94 (From Fat 55); Fat 6g (Saturated 3g);
Cholesterol 19mg; Sodium 8mg; Carbohydrate 8g (Dietary Fiber
1g); Protein 2g.

Cornucopia Cake

If you're eager to incorporate cake into your
Thanksgiving buffet — or if you just want to lay off
the pumpkin pie for a change — this not-too-sweet
confection won't disappoint. Taking some time with
the piped lace design makes it look as if the cornucopia is sitting on a tablecloth.

Tools: *Two 9-inch round cake pans, #2 icing tip, #6
icing tip, #47 icing tip, 6-inch diameter plastic lid*

Preparation time: *20 minutes*

Baking time: *40 minutes plus 30 minutes for cooling*

Decoration time: *1 hour plus 1 hour for refrigeration*

Yield: *12 servings*

Ingredients

For the cake

*1 batch modified Delicious Yellow Cake batter
(see Chapter 2)*

3 teaspoons instant espresso powder

1/2 cup half-and-half

1/2 cup coffee liqueur

For the frosting

1 batch Stiff Decorator Frosting (see Chapter 2)

1 batch Milk Chocolate Frosting (see Chapter 2)

For the decorations

Egg yellow food coloring gel

Harvest brown food coloring gel

Waffle ice cream cone

2 cups Swiss fruits

Directions

Preparing the cake

1 Preheat the oven to 350 degrees F. Grease the cake pans, and line them with parchment paper. Then grease and flour the parchment.

2 Prepare the cake batter as described in Chapter 2, but stir 3 teaspoons instant espresso powder into the sifted flour, and substitute ½ cup half-and-half and ½ cup coffee liqueur for the milk.

3 Bake for 40 minutes, or until a toothpick inserted in the center comes out with moist crumbs attached. Let the cakes cool in the pans for 10 minutes, and then run a knife around the edges. Invert the cakes onto cooling racks.

4 After the cakes are completely cool, torte both cakes so that you have four layers. Frost one layer with milk chocolate frosting, and set the corresponding layer on top. Add a layer of frosting, followed by the third layer, another layer of frosting, and the final layer of cake. Apply a crumb coat (thin layer) of frosting to the entire cake, and refrigerate it for 1 hour.

Decorating the cake

1 Divide and tint the stiff decorator frosting as follows: 2 cups egg yellow and 2 cups harvest brown.

2 Frost the cake with yellow frosting.

3 In the center of the cake, use a toothpick to sketch an oval. Lay the ice cream cone on its side in the center of the oval.

4 Outfit a pastry bag with a coupler, a #47 tip, and brown frosting. Pipe a basket weave design on the ice cream cone cornucopia.

5 Arrange the Swiss fruits so that they appear to tumble out of the cornucopia.

6 Outfit the brown frosting bag with a #6 tip, and pipe an oval border around the, following your previous sketch.

7 Place the 6-inch plastic lid along the sides of the cake and press gently to create an impression of downward arcs. With the #6 tip and brown frosting, pipe little beads along the arcs. Also pipe a row of beads all around the base of the cake.

8 Outfit the brown frosting bag with a #2 tip, and in between the oval and the downward arcs, pipe a lacy design with a pattern of curves and lines.

Cakes and Cookies for Winter Holidays

Wintertime is a great time for baking, and there are plenty of holidays and opportunities for gatherings to treat friends and family to gorgeous cakes and cookies like the ones in this section.

Christmas Tree Cake

This cake for a holiday crowd always draws raves . . . particularly after it's cut and partygoers get a peek at the color inside.

You can play around with your own color scheme for this cake. I like a multicolored approach because it reminds me of vintage Christmas trees decorated with glass ornaments of several different colors.

I like to keep the borders and edges free of any decoration so that the eye is drawn directly to the tree that appears to be standing amidst beautiful, fluffy snow.

Tools: *12-x-18-inch cake pan, bamboo skewer, small rolling pin, #11 icing tip, #100 icing tip, paring knife*

Preparation time: *15 minutes*

Baking time: *50 minutes plus 2 hours for cooling*

Decoration time: *35 minutes plus 1 hour for refrigeration*

Yield: *24 servings*

Ingredients

For the cake

2 batches Red Velvet Cake batter (recipe follows)

For the frosting

2 batches Cream Cheese Frosting (see Chapter 2)

For the decorations

Leaf green food coloring gel

Brown food coloring gel

36 large gumdrops in assorted colors

Large yellow gumdrop

Directions

Preparing the cake

1 Preheat the oven to 350 degrees F. Grease a 12-x-18-inch cake pan, and line it with parchment paper. Then grease and flour the parchment.

2 Prepare the Red Velvet Cake batter according to the recipe that follows. Bake for 50 minutes, or until a toothpick inserted in the center comes out with moist crumbs attached.

3 Let the cake cool in the pan for 10 minutes before inverting it onto a cooling rack. After it is completely cool, apply a crumb coat (thin layer) of cream cheese frosting. Refrigerate for 1 hour.

Decorating the cake

1 Divide and tint the frosting as follows: 2 cups leaf green and ½ cup brown. Frost the cake with the remaining untinted cream cheese frosting.

2 With a bamboo skewer, sketch the shape of a Christmas tree on the surface of the cake. The tree trunk should be 3 inches tall.

3 Outfit a pastry bag with a coupler, #100 tip, and green frosting. Pipe boughs over the tree, over-drawing them for a full, lustrous look if you like. (Make sure to cover up your sketched lines!)

4 Outfit a pastry bag with a coupler, #11 tip, and brown frosting. Pipe the trunk in straight lines. If desired, smooth out the piping with an icing spatula.

5 Place the colored gumdrops on the tree, arranging them to look like ornaments.

6 To create the star, roll out a yellow gumdrop. Either carve out a star shape with a paring knife, or cut the rolled gumdrop into five triangles and form them into a star. Place the star at the top of the tree.

Red Velvet Cake

Preparation time: *15 minutes*

Baking time: *35 minutes*

Ingredients

3¾ cups sifted cake flour

1½ tablespoons cocoa powder

1½ teaspoons salt

1½ teaspoons baking soda

1½ tablespoons white vinegar

2¼ cups granulated white sugar

¾ cup vegetable oil

3 eggs

1½ cups buttermilk

1½ teaspoons pure vanilla extract

2 ounces red food coloring

Directions

1 Preheat the oven to 350 degrees F. Grease and flour a 9-x-13-inch cake pan, and set it aside.

2 In a large bowl, combine the cake flour, cocoa powder, and salt, and whisk them together with a balloon whisk.

3 In a small bowl, dissolve the baking soda in the vinegar. Stir well to make sure the baking soda is fully dissolved.

4 In a large bowl, beat the sugar and oil together until blended. Add the eggs one at a time, beating well after each addition.

5 Add the flour mixture to the sugar and oil mixture in four additions, alternating with the buttermilk. (Begin and end with the flour.) Mix each flour addition just until blended.

6 Beat in the vanilla and food coloring. Stir the baking soda mixture again, and fold it into the batter with a rubber spatula.

7 Bake the cake for 35 minutes, or until a toothpick inserted in the center comes out with moist crumbs attached.

Gingerbread People Cookies

These are great cookies to make with a group because there's something for everyone to do. They can help with rolling the dough, cutting, and decorating. If you want to make cookie ornaments, poke a hole near the top before baking. When cool, string a decorative ribbon through the hole.

Tools: *Gingerbread people cookie cutters*

Preparation time: *1½ hours; includes chilling*

Baking time: *10 minutes*

Yield: *Twelve 6-inch or fourteen 5-inch cookies*

Ingredients

For the cake

3 cups all-purpose flour

1 teaspoon baking soda

¼ teaspoon salt

1 cup light brown sugar

2 teaspoons ground cinnamon

1 tablespoon ground ginger

½ teaspoon ground cloves

½ teaspoon nutmeg, preferably freshly grated

Zest of 1 large orange

¾ cup (1½ sticks) unsalted butter

½ cup unsulphured molasses

1 egg

For the decorations

Currants or raisins

Crystallized ginger chips

Cinnamon candies such as Red Hots (optional)

Royal Icing (see Chapter 2) colored with paste food coloring or powder food coloring (optional)

Directions

1 In the work bowl of a food processor fitted with the steel blade, combine the flour, baking soda, salt, brown sugar, cinnamon, ginger, cloves, nutmeg, and orange zest. Pulse briefly to blend. Cut the butter into small pieces and add to the dry ingredients. Pulse until the butter is cut into very tiny pieces. Add the molasses and egg and process until the mixture forms a ball, about 30 seconds. Wrap the dough tightly in plastic and chill until firm, about 1 hour.

(To make the dough with a mixer and mixing bowl, soften the butter to room temperature and beat until soft and fluffy, about 1 minute. Add the brown sugar and blend together well. Lightly beat the egg and add to the mixture along with the molasses and orange zest. Stop and scrape down the sides of the bowl with a rubber spatula to blend evenly. Combine the flour with the baking soda, salt, cinnamon, ginger, cloves, and nutmeg. Add to the mixture in the mixing bowl in three stages, blending well after each addition. Proceed with the same instructions given for using the food processor.)

2 Preheat the oven to 350 degrees F. Line a cookie sheet with parchment paper.

3 Divide the dough in half and roll each half on a lightly floured surface or between sheets of lightly floured wax paper to about ⅛-inch thick. Gently peel off the wax paper and use a gingerbread person cookie cutter to cut out the dough. Transfer the cookie people to the cookie sheet, leaving 2 inches between them. If using decorations, press raisins, ginger chips, or Red Hots into the shapes to form faces and buttons on the bodies.

4 Bake for 10 to 12 minutes, until firm. Remove the cookie sheet from the oven and transfer the cookies from the parchment paper to cooling racks.

5 If using the Royal Icing to decorate the cookies, wait until they're completely cool. Color the icing with paste or powder food coloring. Place the icing into a parchment paper pastry cone and snip off a small opening at the pointed end. Pipe the icing onto the cookies and leave to set until firm. Store in an airtight container at room temperature for up to a week. Freeze for longer storage.

Per serving *(based on 12 cookies): Calories 331 (From Fat 111); Fat 12g (Saturated 7g); Cholesterol 49mg; Sodium 173mg; Carbohydrate 52g (Dietary Fiber 1g); Protein 4g.*

Heart-O'-Mine Cake

This heart-shaped cake was initially designed for a celebrity's Valentine's Day celebration-for-two. However, where hearts are concerned, any day's the right one to express love.

Candy hearts are part of the decoration for this cake, but you also can make all the decorations with frosting if you have the time.

Tools: *Two 8-inch heart-shaped cake pans, three #7 icing tips*

Preparation time: *20 minutes*

Baking time: *35 minutes plus 1 hour for cooling*

Decoration time: *1¼ hours plus 1 hour for refrigeration*

Yield: *12 servings*

Ingredients

For the cake

1 batch modified Most Excellent White Cake batter (see Chapter 2)

4 ounces white chocolate, chopped

For the frosting

3 batches Buttercream Frosting (see Chapter 2)

For the decorations

Fuchsia food coloring gel

Bright red food coloring gel

Purple food coloring gel

Fuchsia, red, and purple candy hearts

Directions

Preparing the cake

1 Preheat the oven to 350 degrees F, and grease and flour the pans.

2 Prepare the cake batter as described in Chapter 2, but melt 4 ounces of white chocolate into ½ cup of boiling water, cool the mixture, and beat it into the batter after the egg whites and before the flour.

3 Bake the cakes for 35 minutes, or until a toothpick inserted in the center comes out with moist crumbs attached. Let the cakes cool in the pans for 10 minutes before running a knife around the edges. Invert the cakes onto cooling racks.

4 After the cakes are completely cool, level them (see Chapter 3). Frost the top of one cake, stack the other cake on top, and apply a crumb coat (thin layer) of buttercream frosting to the entire cake. Refrigerate it for 1 hour.

Decorating the cake

1 Frost the cake with buttercream, and return it to the refrigerator to chill while you prepare the tinted frosting.

2 Divide and tint the remaining frosting as follows: 1½ cups fuchsia, 1½ cups red, and 1½ cups purple. Outfit three pastry bags — one for each color — with a #7 tip and frosting.

3 Outline the outer edge of the top of the cake with red frosting. Position fuchsia, red, and purple candy hearts all along the top of the cake, sitting just inside the red outline.

4 Pipe stripes along the sides of the cake by alternating the frosting colors.

5 Put a conversation heart in the very center of the cake. Outline the heart in red frosting, then in purple frosting, and finally in fuchsia frosting.

Vary It!: Instead of placing heart-shaped candies around the cake's top border, you can pipe hearts in different colors. To do that, use a #10 icing tip and pipe two facing upside-down teardrops. In lieu of the conversation heart in the center of the cake, you can pipe a message to a special someone. Just keep the script on the small and subtle side.

Baking with molds and cooking spray

Cathedrals, Christmas trees, fire trucks, snowmen, roosters . . . you can get a cake mold in virtually any size, shape, or creation.

If you decide to use a cake mold, take note of its capacity. If you don't have the right amount of batter to fill the mold, the cake doesn't take on the desired shape. And too much batter results in a misshapen cake (and probably a drippy mess in your oven, too).

Before pouring batter into a mold, grease and flour it properly. Many cake molds have intricate designs and patterns that make greasing tricky. To ensure that you get all the crevices, use a nonstick spray with flour.

I first tried cooking spray with flour when I was asked to make a rosebush cake that I designed to include 36 rose cakelets each backed in a very intricate blooming rose-shaped mold. I knew that getting butter into all the crevices of the molds would be an arduous, time-consuming, and ultimately unsuccessful task. A catering friend had mentioned having good results with a cooking spray with flour, so I decided to give it a try. The cakelets tumbled out of the molds perfectly, the molds weren't left sticky, and a new allegiance was born.

Apple & Macs

iPad For Dummies,
2nd Edition
978-1-118-02444-7

iPhone For Dummies,
5th Edition
978-1-118-03671-6

iPod touch For Dummies,
3rd Edition
978-1-118-12960-9

Mac OS X Lion
For Dummies
978-1-118-02205-4

Blogging & Social Media

CityVille For Dummies
978-1-118-08337-6

Facebook For Dummies,
4th Edition
978-1-118-09562-1

Mom Blogging
For Dummies
978-1-118-03843-7

Twitter For Dummies,
2nd Edition
978-0-470-76879-2

WordPress
For Dummies,
4th Edition
978-1-118-07342-1

Business

Cash Flow For Dummies
978-1-118-01850-7

Investing For Dummies,
6th Edition
978-0-470-90545-6

Job Searching
with Social Media
For Dummies
978-0-470-93072-4

QuickBooks 2011
For Dummies
978-0-470-64649-6

Resumes For Dummies,
6th Edition
978-0-470-87361-8

Starting an Etsy Business
For Dummies
978-0-470-93067-0

Cooking & Entertaining

Cooking Basics
For Dummies, 4th Edition
978-0-470-91388-8

Wine For Dummies,
4th Edition
978-0-470-04579-4

Diet & Nutrition

Kettlebells For Dummies
978-0-470-59929-7

Nutrition For Dummies,
5th Edition
978-0-470-93231-5

Restaurant Calorie
Counter For Dummies,
2nd Edition
978-0-470-64405-8

Digital Photography

Digital SLR Cameras &
Photography
For Dummies, 4th Edition
978-1-118-14489-3

Digital SLR Settings
& Shortcuts
For Dummies
978-0-470-91763-3

Photoshop Elements 9
For Dummies
978-0-470-87872-9

Gardening

Gardening Basics
For Dummies
978-0-470-03749-2

Vegetable Gardening
For Dummies,
2nd Edition
978-0-470-49870-5

Green/Sustainable

Raising Chickens
For Dummies
978-0-470-46544-8

Green Cleaning
For Dummies
978-0-470-39106-8

Health

Diabetes
For Dummies,
3rd Edition
978-0-470-27086-8

Food Allergies
For Dummies
978-0-470-09584-3

Living Gluten-Free
For Dummies,
2nd Edition
978-0-470-58589-4

Hobbies

Beekeeping
For Dummies,
2nd Edition
978-0-470-43065-1

Chess For Dummies,
3rd Edition
978-1-118-01695-4

Drawing For Dummies,
2nd Edition
978-0-470-61842-4

eBay For Dummies,
7th Edition
978-1-118-09806-6

Knitting
For Dummies,
2nd Edition
978-0-470-28747-7

Language &
Foreign Language

English Grammar
For Dummies,
2nd Edition
978-0-470-54664-2

French For Dummies,
2nd Edition
978-1-118-00464-7

German For Dummies,
2nd Edition
978-0-470-90101-4

Spanish Essentials
For Dummies
978-0-470-63751-7

Spanish For Dummies,
2nd Edition
978-0-470-87855-2